COOL
CLAY
CREATIONS

This edition published in 2016
By SpiceBox™
12171 Horseshoe Way
Richmond, BC
Canada V7A 4V4

First published in 2013
Copyright © SpiceBox™ 2013

ISBN 10: 1-77132-068-0
ISBN 13: 978-1-77132-068-9

CEO and Publisher: Ben Lotfi
Editorial: Ania Jaraczewski
Creative Director: Garett Chan
Art Director: Christine Covert
Design, Illustration & Photography: Charmaine Muzyka
Production: James Badger, Mell D'Clute
Sourcing: Tony Su, May Ko
Special thanks to Charmaine Muzyka, Kirsten Reddecopp, Christine
Covert, Garett Chan, Mell D'Clute and Ania Jaraczewski for creating the
clay characters pictured in this book; and to our young models, Ashley
Landsiedel, Selma Dzumhura, Jennifer Blanco, and Bryan Ormandy.

For more SpiceBox products and information, visit our website:
www.spiceboxbooks.com

Manufactured in China

5 7 9 10 8 6 4

Contents

Projects:

page 14

page 28

page 32

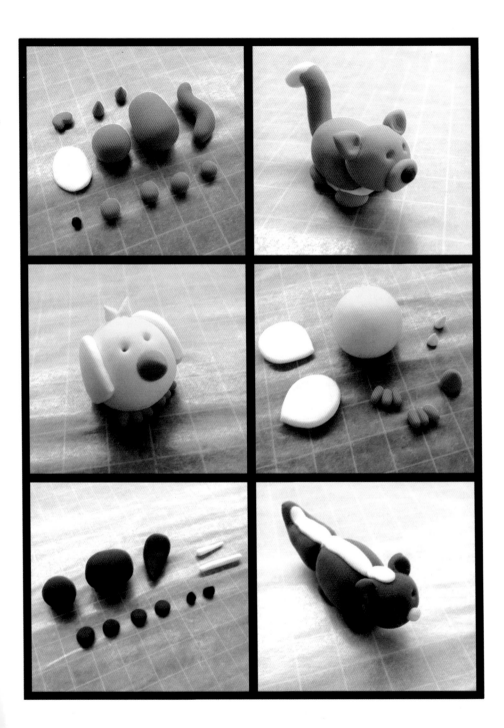

Introduction

Clay can be magically transformed from muddy earth into all sorts of amazing things. It's no wonder people have been using it for about 26,000 years, and still do! It's one of the world's oldest art materials—the very first things people made out of clay were figurines of humans and animals, kind of like the ones in this book!

The earliest clay objects were sculpted and then left to dry in the sun until they hardened. Doesn't that sound easy? Air-drying clay also hardens on its own so you don't have to bake it. It's fun and easy to use! Better still, it comes in lots of great colors. Try out a few of the projects in the book and then let your imagination take over and come up with your own awesome creations!

Clay sure has come a long way since I was made! Today, you can even make animated films with moveable clay characters!

Ancient Mayan Statue

Tools & Materials

Cool Clay

Air-drying clay will harden on its own after you've finished molding it. And it will still look exactly the way you made it!

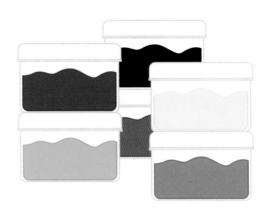

Parchment Paper

Not that you would *ever* make a mess, but it's still a good idea to put parchment paper or a plastic mat over your work surface. This will also keep your projects from picking up dirt so your creatures won't all turn into dust bunnies!

Dowel

The clay is pretty sticky and might stick to wood. To roll it out, either use a plastic dowel or cover the clay with parchment paper if using a wooden rolling pin.

Shaping Tools

You can make little holes and lines using different tools. Check out my nifty seams— they were made with the pointy tool!

Fun Extras

You can give your creatures loads of personality by using fun pre-made body parts and accessories like feet, eyes and hats. These are easy to attach—just stick the tabs into your creation while it's still soft. Or you can wait till it dries and glue the pieces on afterward.

Tips & Techniques

Before You Start

Here are a few tips that every clay artist should read before they embark on their clay-making adventures:

Don't eat the clay, even if you're making yummy-looking food out of it! Even though this clay is non-toxic, make sure to keep it away from pets and younger siblings.

I see those crumbs on your fingers! Unless you want them to become part of your project, you'd better wash your hands first! I'm watching you!

You don't want your clay drying out before your masterpiece is finished, so make sure you keep whatever you're not using in a plastic bag or container. Only take out small bits at a time.

If the clay does start to feel dry, all is not lost! Work a few drops of water into it until it's easy to mold again.

actual size pair of eyes:

● ●

All the creations in this book were made using very small amounts of clay. A little goes a long way!

Techniques

Soften it Up

Kneed the clay for a minute or so to make it soft and easy to use.

Mixing Colors

Don't have the color you need? Don't worry! You can mix two or more colors together to make any color you want. Just add small bits of color together and work the clay until you get the shade you want. If you want stripes or swirls, mix the clay just a little bit, so you can still see the different colors.

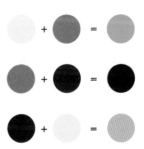

Go Wild!

Because you don't have to bake the clay, you can stick all kinds of things into it: beads, buttons, twigs, fabric, sparkles, bits of wire and pipe cleaners. Once the clay has dried, you can also paint or draw on it. Be creative!

Tips & Techniques

Simple Shapes

The characters and objects in the book may look hard to make, but they were all put together from very simple shapes—like a round ball for a body and flat circles for ears. Easy! Each project will show you which shapes you need. It's a good idea to make all the shapes before you start sticking them together. That way it's easier to make sure that each shape is the right size.

Making a Teardrop Shape

Many of the projects in this book use "teardrop" shapes. To make this shape, first roll the clay into a ball. Then pinch out one end and roll that end back and forth a few times until you have a shape that looks like a drop of water.

Hey, who are you calling **round**?

Drying Time

Once you've finished your project, leave it to dry for at least 24 hours. Then your cool clay creation is done!

How to Make Your Own Air-Drying Clay

If you run out of clay, you can make your own homemade version!
Ask an adult to help you.

Ingredients:

1 cup cornstarch

2 cups baking soda

1¼ cups cold water

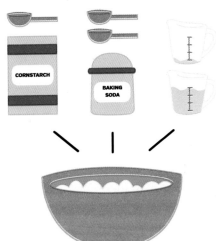

Directions:

Step 1: Combine cornstarch, baking soda and water in a saucepan.

Step 2: Cook for 5 minutes at medium heat, stirring the whole time.

Step 3: Remove from heat. Put clay on a sheet of waxed paper.
Once cool, kneed for 5 minutes.

Step 4: Once you've molded it into a creation, it will take 48 hours to
1 week to dry. Then you can paint it!

Projects

Sallee the Starfish

Sallee lives in the sea with her underwater friends. Try making a whole cluster of sea stars in different colors!

Step 1: Make 5 teardrop shapes. Flatten them out with your finger and bend the tips slightly.

Step 2: Join the teardrop shapes into a circle by sticking them together at the wider ends.

Step 3: Make a ball and flatten it into a circle. Press the circle into the center of the starfish to keep all the pieces together.

Step 4: Make 2 white circles for the eyes and press them into the middle circle.

Step 5: Make 2 black circles for the pupils and press them into the eyes.

Step 6: Make a bunch of little circles in a different color and stick them onto the arms of the starfish for decoration.

Here are some of Sallee's friends:

Cal the Caterpillar

Cal is a bit shy, and usually hides in the garden under a pile of leaves. You can make him all green, rainbow-colored or stripey!

Step 1: Roll out 8 balls for the body, each one slightly larger than the last.

Step 2: Make 2 small white circles for the eyes and 2 tiny black ones for the pupils.

Step 3: Starting with the smallest body ball, begin attaching the pieces together.

Step 4: Attach the balls together so that Cal's body is curved as shown. His head should be raised.

Step 5: Add the eyes on either side of the largest ball.

Step 6: Add the pupils and you're finished!

Here are some of Cal's friends:

Bella the Bird

Bella perches in the treetops when she's not flying around. You can make all kinds of different birds, including penguins, ducks, owls and parrots.

feathers: beak: toes:

Step 1: Make a yellow ball for Bella's body.

Step 2: Make 2 yellow teardrop shapes for feathers. Using orange, make a teardrop shape for the beak, and 6 little cylinders for toes.

Step 3: Put 3 of the toes together and press down at one end so they stick together. Do the same with the other 3.

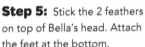

Step 4: Make 2 white teardrop shapes and flatten them for wings.

Step 5: Stick the 2 feathers on top of Bella's head. Attach the feet at the bottom.

Step 6: Attach the beak and wings. Poke 2 little holes for eyes.

Some of Bella's feathery friends:

Peggy the Pig

Peggy lives on a farm with all her animal pals, including cows, sheep, chickens and horses. You can make them all out of clay for a barnyard scene!

Step 1: Make a ball out of light pink clay for Peggy's body.

Step 2: Make a smaller ball with dark pink clay. Flatten it slightly to make a snout.

Step 3: Make 2 flat ears with dark pink clay.

Step 4: Roll out 4 round little feet and a curly tail with dark pink clay.

Step 5: Stick the ears onto the top of the body. Press the snout onto the front and the tail onto the back.

Step 6: Fold the tops of the ears down. Attach the feet to the bottom of the pig. Poke 2 little holes for eyes and 2 holes for nostrils. Oink oink!

Some of Peggy's farmyard friends:

Stellar Spaceship

Explore space without leaving home, with this futuristic rocket ship! Then make some UFOs and weird-looking aliens to complete your space scene.

Step 1: Roll out an egg shape for the body of the ship. Flatten it slightly with your finger.

Step 2: Roll out a smaller egg shape. Flatten it to make the domed window.

Step 3: Make 2 white or gray wings.

Step 4: Make 2 flat, triangular pieces for the fins, and some circular white pieces for lights.

Step 5: Attach the wings to the bottom of the body. Stick the window on top.

Step 6: Add the fins and lights, and you're ready to blast off!

Some aliens and spaceships you might see on your journey through space:

Lenny the Lizard

Lenny is a desert creature who loves the sun. Try giving him multi-colored spots or wild stripes!

Step 1: Roll out an oval for Lenny's body. Pinch and roll out one side of the oval to get the tail.

Step 2: Make an oval for the head and flatten one end for the nose.

Step 3: Make 12 little toes. Take 3 at a time and press down at one end so they stick together.

Step 4: Make a bunch of small circles for the spots, and 2 small black circles for eyes.

Step 5: Attach the head to the front of Lenny's body. Attach the feet to the bottom so they stick out to the sides.

Step 6: Speckle Lenny's body with spots. Stick the black circles on for eyes, and poke 2 small holes for nostrils.

Here are some of Lenny's friends:

Frank the Fox

Frank lives in the forest with a bunch of his woodland pals. Try creating a scene with twigs and leaves for Frank and his friends.

Step 1: Make an orange oval shape for the body.

head: belly:

Step 2: Make an orange ball for the head. Then make a white ball and roll it out to make a flat oval for the belly.

feet:

ears: snout:

nose:

Step 3: Make 4 balls for the feet, a flattened bean shape for the snout and 2 flat teardrop shapes for ears. Make a tiny black ball for the tip of Frank's nose.

Step 4: Make two pieces for the tail: a small white ball and an orange cylinder. Stick them together and roll them until they form a single piece.

Step 5: Stick the belly piece onto the body piece. Then attach the head to the body on one end, and the tail on the other end.

Step 6: Add the feet, ears, snout and nose as shown. Then poke two little holes for eyes.

Here are some of Frank's friends:

Racecar

Make a bunch of racecars in different colors. Then construct a racetrack using paper and markers, so you and your friends can see whose car is the fastest!

Step 1: Make an oval shape for the body of the car. Flatten one side against a flat surface.

Step 2: Make a black ball for the driver's helmet. Stick a flat white rectangle on it for the visor.

Step 3: Make a rectangle for the rear spoiler, and two small cylinders for a frame. Roll out a small strip of clay to form into a number for the top of the spoiler.

Step 4: Make 2 small black balls for the front wheels and flatten them slightly. Make 2 slightly larger tires for the back wheels.

Step 5: Make 2 stripes and lay them across the body of the car.

Step 6: Attach the wheels to the bottom of the car and the helmet to the top. Stick the spoiler onto the back with a cylinder propping it up on either side. Now see how fast you can make it go!

Some more cars for inspiration:

Danny the Dinosaur

Danny and his dinosaur friends lived a long, long time ago! Make a few different dinosaurs and watch them roam the jungle once more.

spots:

horn: spikes:

Step 1: Make an oval shape. Pinch and roll out one side of the oval to get the tail.

Step 2: Make a smaller egg shape for the head. Then made a ball and flatten it to make Danny's neck frill.

Step 3: Use different colors to make a bunch of small flat circles for spots, a teardrop shape for a horn, and little triangles for spikes.

eyes:

feet:

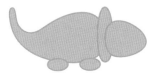

Step 4: Roll 4 small balls for feet. Then make 2 small white circles for eyes, and 2 smaller black circles for pupils.

Step 5: Attach the neck frill to the body and then attach the head to the frill. Press the feet onto the bottom of the body.

Step 6: Press the horn onto Danny's forehead and attach all the spikes and spots. Using your tools, press some wrinkles into the frill and poke in some nostrils and a mouth.

Here are some of Danny's dino friends:

Eddy the Teddy Bear

Teddy bears make great buddies. And Eddy makes the perfect gift to give to a friend or someone special!

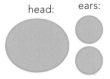

head: ears:

snout: eyes: nose:

Step 1: Make a ball for Eddy's body.

Step 2: Make a slightly smaller ball for the head. Make 2 little balls and flatten them for the ears.

Step 3: Make a flat oval shape for Eddy's snout, and a smaller black oval for his nose. Make two little black circles for eyes.

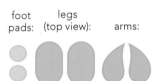

foot pads: legs (top view):   arms:

Step 4: Roll out a pair of cylinders for legs, and a flat pair of circles for footpads. Roll out two more cylinders and make each of them narrower at one end, for arms.

Step 5: Attach Eddy's arms and legs to his body. Then press the snout, nose, eyes and ears onto the head as shown.

Step 6: With a pointy tool, poke some holes down Eddy's middle for seams, then give him whiskers. Press in some lines for the mouth, paws and ears.

Here are some of Eddy's friends:

Peter the Puppy

Peter likes long walks and a good scratch behind the ears. He'd be especially happy if you made him a nice, juicy bone to chew on.

ears:

feet:

back legs:

tail:

Step 1: Make a brown ball for Peter's body and a slightly smaller egg shape for his head.

Step 2: Make 2 flat ovals for ears and 2 small balls for feet.

Step 3: Roll out 2 cylinders for his hind legs. Make a smaller cylinder for a tail.

Step 4: Attach the head to the body. Then attach the ears to the top of the head and fold them over.

Step 5: Attach the nose, tail, front paws and back legs.

Step 6: Using your tools, poke two holes for eyes and press some lines into Peter's feet for paws. If you want, you can give him some spots too.

Here are some of Peter's friends:

Ronnie the Robot

Ronnie was created in a robotics lab. The scientists gave him a heart so he would feel like a person!

Step 1: Make 1 larger cube and 1 smaller cube for Ronnie's body and head.

Step 2: Make 4 balls for feet and hands. Then make 2 thin cylinders for arms, and 2 shorter cylinders for legs.

Step 3: Make 2 small white circles for eyes, and 2 smaller black circles for pupils. Form a small heart using two flat teardrop shapes.

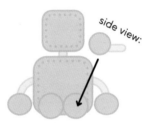

side view:

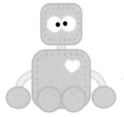

Step 4: Attach the head to the body with a small ball. Poke a bunch of little holes around the edges to make it look like Ronnie has screws holding him together.

Step 5: Attach the hands to the arms and the arms to the body. Attach the feet to the legs and the legs to the body.

Step 6: Press the white circles onto Ronnie's face, and then the black circles on top. Put the heart on his chest, and Ronnie is ready!

Some of Ronnie's pals:

Marcus the Monster

Marcus lives under your bed—augh! He's not so bad, though, just look at those big round eyes…er, eye.

Step 1: Make a round ball for Marcus' body.

ears: feet: arms:

Step 2: Make 2 flattened ovals for ears, 2 small balls for feet and 2 teardrop shapes for arms.

teeth:

eye:

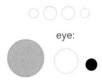

Step 3: Make 4 very small circles for teeth. You'll need 4 circles for his eye: 1 large orange one, 1 medium white, 1 small black and 1 tiny white.

Step 4: Attach the ears to the top of the body and the feet to the bottom. Attach the arms by pressing the narrow ends onto the body.

Step 5: Attach the large orange circle for the eye and make a large indent for the mouth.

Step 6: Place the medium white circle, the black circle and the tiny white circle to make the eye as shown. Press the teeth into the mouth indent.

Here are some of Marcus' monster friends:

Manny the Monkey

Manny will do anything to get his paws on some bananas! After you've made him, mold a bunch of bananas for him to eat.

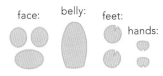

Step 1: Make a large brown ball for Manny's body, and a slightly smaller one for his head. Make a curved cylinder for a tail.

Step 2: Make two brown ovals for his legs, and two brown arms that are pinched at the top. Make 2 round pink ears and 2 black eyes.

Step 3: Using pink, make two circles and an oval for the face, and a large oval that's flattened at one end for the belly. Make 2 balls for feet and 2 for hands.

Step 4: Attach the belly to the body, flat end on bottom. Then attach the head and legs. Attach the arms with the pinched end at the top.

Step 5: First press the two circles onto the middle of the face, and then place the oval over the lower parts of the circles as shown. Attach the hands and feet.

Step 6: Attach the tail and the eyes. Poke two holes for nostrils and then give him a mischievous smile.

Here are some of Manny's friends:

Hazel the Witch

Hazel loves Halloween! With her jack o' lanterns and black bat, she's ready for some spooky fun.

Step 1: Make a green ball for the head and a larger black one for the witch's body.

Step 2: For the hat brim, make a black ball and flatten it out till it's wider than the head. Make a teardrop shape to go on top, and a flat yellow strip for the trim.

Step 3: Make 2 green balls for the hands, 2 yellow balls for the buttons, a small green ball for the nose and a tiny green ball for the wart.

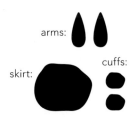

Step 4: For the skirt, take a lump of black clay and flatten it so the edges are uneven. Do the same with 2 small lumps for the sleeve cuffs. Make 2 arms that are pinched at the top.

Step 5: Attach the head to the body. Make the hat by pressing the black teardrop onto the hat brim. Attach the arms to the sides of the body, the cuffs to the ends of the arms and the skirt to the bottom of the body.

Step 6: Stick the buttons onto the front of the body and press the hands onto the sleeve cuffs. Place the trim around the hat and press the hat onto Hazel's head. Attach the nose and wart. Poke in eyes and a mouth. Boo!

Here are some other Halloween ideas:

Steve the Snowman

Even if there's no snow outside, you can still build a snowman! You can make Steve entirely out of clay or use real buttons, a bit of fabric for a scarf and twigs for arms.

Step 1: Make a large white ball for the body and a slightly smaller one for the head.

Step 2: Take 8 small white balls and 8 small red balls and put them in a row. Roll them all together to form the scarf.

Step 3: For the hat brim, flatten a small black ball until it's wider than the head. Make a cylinder for the top of the hat and a red strip for the trim.

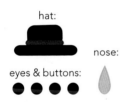

hat:

nose:

eyes & buttons:

Step 4: Attach the cylinder to the hat brim and wrap the red strip around it. Make 4 small balls for eyes and buttons, and a small orange teardrop shape for the nose.

Step 5: Wrap the scarf around Steve where his head and body meet. Stick the end of the scarf to the side of his body.

Step 6: Press the 2 eyes onto the face, and the 2 buttons onto the body. Attach the nose to the face and carve in a little smile.

Here are some other Christmas ideas:

Berry Good

You can make a whole miniature fruit bowl, or you can mold the top stem of each fruit into a loop and turn it into a fun pendant to wear.

Step 1: Make an egg shape with red clay and flatten it slightly on your work surface.

Step 2: Make 2 teardrops for the leaves and a small cylinder for the stem.

Step 3: Make 6 tiny white balls for the strawberry's seeds.

Step 4: Press the stem into the top end of the berry.

Step 5: Stick the wide end of the leaves into the base of the strawberry stem.

Step 6: Stick the seeds onto the berry. With a straight-edged tool, press a thin line into each leaf for veins.

Some other fruity ideas:

Sweet Peas

Even if you don't like eating all the vegetables on your dinner plate, you'll love making these cute little peas!

Step 1: Form a large dark green teardrop shape.

Step 2: Flatten the teardrop out with a dowel. This will be the pea pod.

Step 3: Using a lighter green, roll 4 balls in various sizes.

Step 4: Put the peas on the flattened pod.

Step 5: Fold up the edges of the pod so it sticks to the sides of the peas.

Step 6: Make some little holes for eyes and you're done!

Some other veggies to make:

Small Sushi

Making real sushi can be pretty challenging, but these tiny sushi rolls are a snap to put together!

Step 1: For the rice, make 18-24 little oval balls out of white clay and lay them down in 2 rows so that they all stick together.

Step 2: Make some oval shapes in different colors for the sushi fillings.

Step 3: Using black clay, make a thin strip of "seaweed" long enough to wrap around the fillings once.

Step 4: Group your fillings together as shown.

Step 5: Wrap the seaweed around your fillings. If the strip is too long, simply cut off the end.

Step 6: Wrap the rice strip around the outside of the roll. Place the sushi upright and press the top down to flatten the fillings.

Some delicious inspiration:

Piece of Cake

This yummy mini slice of birthday cake would make the perfect decoration for a birthday card or gift wrap.

icing: candle:

Step 1: Using yellow clay, make 2 thick triangles for the cake. The triangles should have two long sides and a short side.

Step 2: Using brown clay, make 2 thin triangles for the icing. Also make one rectangle that's long enough to cover the short side of the triangles.

Step 3: Using white clay, make a small cylinder for a candle and little teardrop shapes for icing. Make a teardrop-shaped yellow flame.

Step 4: Press the triangles together as shown, alternating between yellow and brown.

Step 5: Attach your decorative icing to one end.

Step 6: Press the brown rectangle onto the short side of the cake. Stick the candle on top. Mmmm!

Some delicious inspiration:

Flower Power

It's never the wrong time of year for spring flowers when you can make them out of clay! These cute flowers are a great gift idea.

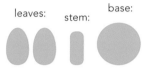

leaves: stem: base:

Step 1: Make 4 red ovals and flatten them to make flower petals.

Step 2: Make 2 green ovals and flatten them for leaves. Make a cylinder stem and a flattened green circle for the base.

Step 3: Attach the stem to the center of the base.

Step 4: Attach 2 petals to the top of the stem, one on either side.

Step 5: Attach the other 2 petals so that they overlap the first two slightly.

Step 6: Add your 2 leaves to the base of the stem and you're finished!

Some other flowers to try:

Bouncy Balls

Objects made out of air-drying clay actually bounce! You can also make marbles by mixing different colors together to get stripes and swirls.

Step 1: Roll out a ball in any color.

Step 2: Using a different color, make 8 teardrop shapes and then flatten them to make petals.

Step 3: Make several little balls for the middle of the flower and to decorate the rest of the ball.

Step 4: Press 4 of the flower petals onto one side of the ball so they stick together at their wider ends. Do the same on the other side of the ball.

Step 5: Add a yellow ball in the center of each flower.

Step 6: Decorate around the flowers with the rest of the little balls.

Some more bouncy balls and marbles to try:

Doughnut Pendant

Mmmm…doughnuts! Make this fun, colorful pendant, and then try designing a matching ring, or a bracelet with doughnut beads.

side view:

Step 1: Make a thick, flat cylinder.

Step 2: Make thin layer of light pink for the icing.

Step 3: Make a bunch of tiny little balls for sprinkles.

Step 4: Cover the doughnut with the icing. Take a pen or pencil and stick it through the middle to make a hole. Smooth out any rough edges at the bottom.

Step 5: Decorate it with sprinkes! For extra detail, take a pin and poke tiny holes in all the sprinkles.

Step 6: Stick a metal ring partway into the doughnut and carefully pinch the clay back together in that spot. Once the clay has dried, you can attach your pendant to a chain.

Some more jewelry projects to try:

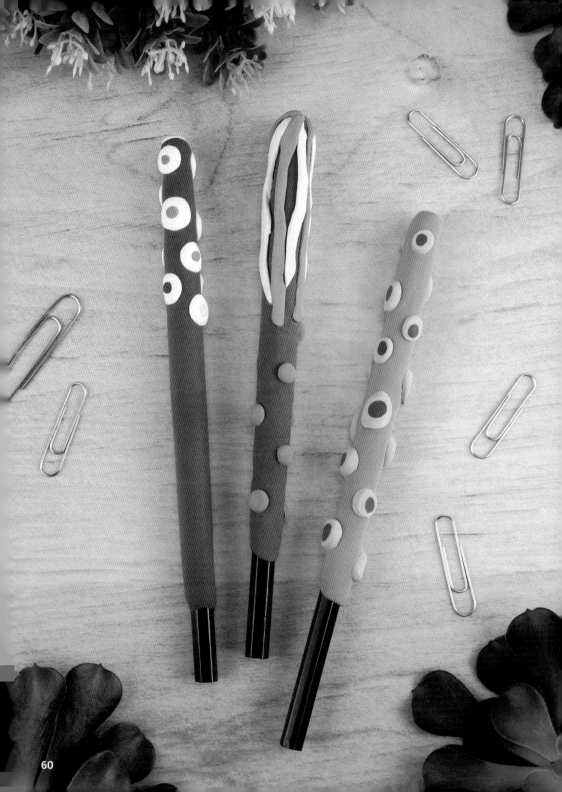

Pencil Fashion

Use clay to decorate your school supplies to make them colorful and unique. Be the envy of all your classmates!

Step 1: Make a large rectangle and flatten it with your dowel.

Step 2: Roll out 10–15 little balls for decoration.

Step 3: Roll out some yellow and orange strips.

Step 4: Cover most of your pen or pencil with the clay rectangle. Cut off any extra clay.

Step 5: Decorate one half of the pen or pencil with the little balls.

Step 6: Press the orange and yellow strips down on the other half to make flames. Now you can study in style!

You can roll it, squeeze it, poke it, flatten it, press it and cut it to create anything you want!

whoo whooooo

doesn't like to play with clay?